"By Land...

JOHN BURGESS

Also by John Burgess:
Graffito
A History of Guns in the Family
Punk Poems

Acknowledgements:
Thanks to David Lasky for instruction and technical assist; Daris Swindler for "A Most Perfect View"; and Patsy Burgess for going along.

Support small presses
and independent bookstores.
–jb

Copyright©John Burgess 2015
www.punkpoet.net

ISBN: 978-0-9905265-3-7
LCCN: 2015930527

Published by:
Ravenna Press (ravennapress.com)
Washington State

For you whom I meant along the way.

Key

*I marked my name on a large pine tree
immediately on the isthmus
William Clark December 3rd 1805.
By Land from the U. States
in 1804 & 1805.*

Blues. Song of American origin, that takes the basic form, often improvised in performance, of a 12-bar chorus (*Webster's*); gives voice to Sacagawea, York and Lewis; written for harmonica and fiddle.

Course & Distance. Essay in 10 fragments; explores personal intersections with the Lewis & Clark Trail; title from the daily mapmaking field notes taken by Wm. Clark.

Dispatch. Graphic poems; title and font from the flag of the *St. Louis Post-Dispatch*.

Inventory. Handwritten lists; misspellings and illegibility are my own.

Joke. From L. *jocus* word-play; cf. G. *jucks, jux* joke, spree, and Du. *jok* jest (*The Oxford Dictionary of English Etymology*).

Lewis & Clark among the Indians. Concrete poems; typed on a c.1966 Smith-Corona Super Sterling; title and found words from *Lewis & Clark among the Indians*, James P. Ronda.

Map & Text. Marks the major arc of the narrative; follows chronologically the places where I intersected with the Lewis & Clark Trail: 1) Montana, 2) Pacific Coast, and 3) St. Louis.

Notes. Lines salvaged from my notebooks; used as imaginary footnotes to a fictional academic text with made-up chapter titles that imply narrative structure; all notes are true.

Riff. A jazz term referring to a melodic and often constantly repeated phrase (*Webster's*); retains spelling from the *Definitive Journals of Lewis & Clark* and other source texts.

Sonnet. 14-line reconstructions using words and phrases found in the journal entries of Wm. Clark; retains the Captain's original spelling and phrasing.

Substitution. As the title implies, updates passages by substituting words to imply parallel context; retains original spelling and phrasing from the Journals.

Travels in North America. Erasure poems using found travel-book phrases, from *Fielding's Lewis & Clark Trail*; title from a book noted at the *Reconstruction of Thomas Jefferson's Library* exhibit at the Library of Congress, Washington, D.C.

Montana

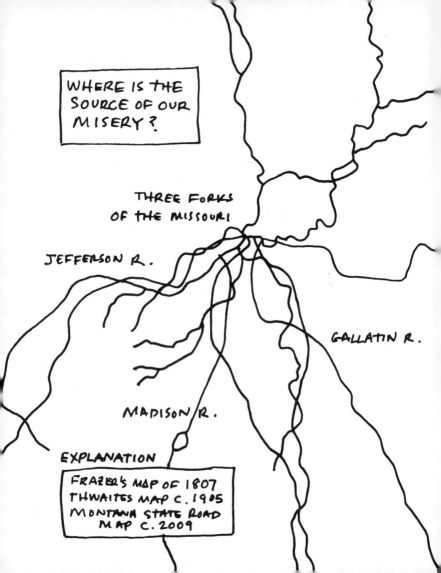

(for this is) destiny / proximity / history / misery.

Retrieval is an active investigative effort to recreate facts based on fragments.

You either expect rhyme and regular rhythm, or you don't; you either expect narrative or you don't.

Acts remain uncountable, as continuous landscape, as infinite movement, all muscle and manifest.

The passage of time inexorably leads to a weakening of events and facts that were once clear and chock-full of specifics.

(for this is) interrelatedness / incompleteness / forgetfulness.

3 examples: a) you fight the fish so you can fight the hook; b) shovels leave clumps of dirt on March snow; c) I forget that surveyors were working nearby.

We often feel sympathy, irony and discomfort as onlookers at historical sites.

To stand in this place, in wide emptiness, to last in this space, where you feel so vast.

Memory as combustible as August grass.

Camped near Three Forks, Montana, 2010.08.02-06.

Inventory

What Th. Jefferson authorized the Secretary of War to provide for the Corps, c. June 1803

instruments for ascertaining the geography, light articles for barter, & presents among the Indians, arms for 10 to 12 men, boats, tents, & other traveling apparatus, ammunition, medicine, surgical instruments, provisions,

Inventory

What I packed by trunk to Montana,
c. 1978

Men's briefs, socks, wool socks, jeans,
t-shirts, sweatshirt, Pendleton shirt,
toque, denim jacket blanket-lined,
Thinsulate long underwear, Portable
Nietzsche, Journals of Lewis & Clark,
On Being & Nothingness, Emily Dickinson
Complete, Mark Twain Roughing It,
ceremonial dress pants, collared
shirt + belt, cut-offs, runners,
Red Wing work boots, pocket-sized
transistor radio, notebook lined,

Travels in North America

On your trek west it is interesting to see
_____. To get a good view of the
_____, drive _____ from the
_____, and turn _____ on Highway
_____. A _____ marks the site where
_____ was found.

Course & Distance #01

I'm on my knees. It's noon and August and already 80 in the Valley. It's a small cemetery not more than an acre or so, square with a circle drive through its heart. While there are wheat fields adjacent, there is a subdivision less than a quarter mile away – land that Survco subdivided in the late 1970s now paved streets and ranch-style houses in covenant colors. There are two men working in the cemetery, one standing at a transit. They're locating / relocating plots, marking a field map.

I use a jackknife to cut away the needle-and-thread grass that has overgrown the flat gravestone. I look up from time to time, reckon where the Gallatin flows; somewhere near I sense – perhaps that line of trees past where those houses are now. The valley is hazed from a summer forest fire burning at the far end of the range toward the wilderness area. I keep at it until I reestablish its borders.

Sonnet

the low or overflown
points

>> or bottom lands
>> of the groth of
>> Cotton & Willow

the high bottom of
rich fertile Soils

or the Clouds
Guilded in the most
beautiful manner

>> Blue & white streaks
>> Centering at the sun
>> as She disappeared or

near falling from the Pancelia of rocks

Sonnet

to lay by at this place to

        fix the Lattitude & Longitude to

    correct cronometer

    run down Sunday

to walk out   to view
those remarkable places
    the Countrey
    thro which I
    passed
    this day

to be reminded

                                    in this place

to be obsvd.

                                  of your grace

Joke

in St. Louis the Captains go
to this brothel for the first time

they end up in line behind a Frenchman

DISPATCH

Tacked inside the lid of his trunk was a red pennant, machine-sewn with birds & landmarks.

DISPATCH

The Captains carried with them their Chief in obverse.

SMALLER THAN ACTUAL SIZE

DISPATCH

Delivery was unreliable with his messages arriving often weeks or months later.

MONTICELLO →

Lewis & Clark among the Indians

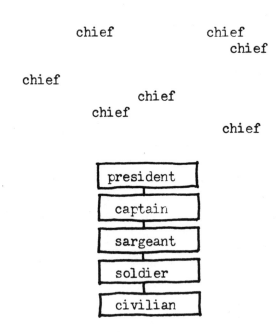

Travels in North America

The best way north from _____ is to cross the river to _____ and then turn right on U.S. Highway ____. The drive from _____ to _____ is beautiful, regardless of whether you're on the north or south side of the river. Today, if you look for _____, you'll find _____.

Course & Distance #02

It's 2,156.6 miles from Watertown NY, where I was born in 1958, to the Three Forks of the Missouri River. After a slight southwesterly course, the map shows a relatively straight course across the Great Plains into the Big Sky country.

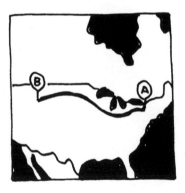

The result is a location with a more northerly latitude, 43° 97' N to 45° 56' N, where each degree of latitude at 45° is approx. 49 miles. Lewis mistakenly located Three Forks at 45° 23' 34" N. In 1978 it is still by at least 100 miles the farthest north I have ever lived.

Joke

a lawyer, a politician, and the Captains are in a pirogue

the politician asks who's doing the poling here

Riff

i.
a verry large Snake was killed to day
Sunning himself on the bank

we killed a large rattle Snake near our Camp—
saw several in the course of a day

I walked this morning on Shore & Saw Several
rattle Snakes on the Plain, the wind from the SW

a snake which resembles the rattle Snake
his colour Some thing like a rattle Snake

ii.
In walking on Shore I Saw Several rattle Snakes
and narrowly escaped at two different times

was very near being bitten twice
but luckley escaped being bit

as also the Squar when walking with
her husband on Shore—

was near being bit by a rattle Snake between
his legs as he was fishing on the Shore

iii.
Saw rattle Snakes but verry little timber
Saw a number of rattle Snakes and killed one

I was out hunting this morning
and killed a rattlesnake among the rocks

one mile past a rock at the N. side where
the pictures of the Devil and other things

We kild 3 Rattel Snakes at that Rock
and Saved the Skin

Course & Distance #03

There are four objects that belonged to my dad that I now pack with me place to place:

1. Rawhide hunting hat, [i] worn deer hunting. Originally passing to my Uncle Joe, for 33 years, before being mailed to me in 2011 via USPS.

---

i. Among the provisions for the Expedition were 15 Match Coats, 15 Priv. Blue Wool Overalls, 36 Pairs Stockings, 20 Frocks, 30 Priv. lin. Shirts, 20 Priv. Shoes, 1 pk. Hhd.

2. Plum bob (or plummet), used while land surveying.[ii] Obtained during upstate N.Y. visit c. 1978. Traveled in luggage transcontinental, including plane change in Denver.

---

ii. There is no plummet in the equipage used by Lewis & Clark to take observations. Here's the list as noted by Lewis:
    1st – a brass Sextant of 10 Inches radius
    2nd – A common octant of 14 inches radius
    3rd 4th 5th – An Artificial Horizon [of three Variants]
    6th – A Chronometer
    7th – A Circumferentor, circle 6 inches diameter

3. Triangle used for drafting [iii] post-survey maps showing metes and bounds. Kept among pens and rulers since the mid-1970s.

---

iii. Clark's plotting instruments were supplemented with 14 bags of Parchment of 2 bu., 100 Quils, 6 Brass Inkstands, 6 Papers Ink Powder, 1/4 lb. Indian ink.

4. Replica Kentucky flintlock long rifle, [iv] crafted by Jack Perry c. 1968. Transported, along with great aunt's trunk, to Montana by automobile c. 1980, then by trailer to the coast c. 1984.

---

iv. There were 15 Kentucky rifles listed in the inventory purchased for the expedition by Lewis in 1803. Editors note states: presumably the Kentucky volunteers provided their own rifles.

Notes: *"Packing and leaving ..."*

1. Concurrent with "I slept thru (the) lunar eclipse last night" the Journalist's dream notebook entry dated "early a.m. March 3rd" indicates he was at the time dreaming of bear. His face being covered at the time with what he describes as a "bear'd."

2. Notebook entry "I observed a great number of Dark Geese this evening" is most likely referencing *Branta candensis* identified by "largely dark plumage." By the end of the 20th Century the more commonly called "Canada goose" had a sprawling urban presence of which the Journalist would have certainly been aware.

Lewis & Clark among the Indians

4600 sewing needles
500 brooches 8 ket-
tles 1800 fish hooks
hawkbells thimbles
11 dozen knives ruf-
fled shirts blue beads
brass buttons mocca-
sin awls medals flags

guns
powder
shot

Substitution

for Indian(s), substitute Republican(s)

i.
matters being thus arranged I directed the fiddle
to be played & the party danced very merrily
much to the amusement of the <u>Republicans</u>

ii.
I must confess that the state of my own mind at
this moment did not well accord w/ the
prevailing mirth as I somewhat feared the caprice
of the <u>Republicans</u> ... I determined to keep the
<u>Republicans</u> in a good humour if possible

iii.
the ornaments of each <u>Republican</u> are Similar,
Such as large blue & white beads, either pendant
from their ears or encircling their necks or wrists

& arm, <u>Republicans</u> also ware bracelets of Brass,
Copper & horn, & trinkets of Shells, Fish Bones
& curious feathers

iv.
those <u>Republicans</u> are much pleased with my
black Servent—<u>Republican</u> womin verry fond of
caressing our men

v.
the gun we took w/ us, I also retook the flagg but
left the medal about the neck of the dead
<u>Republican</u> that they might be informed who we
were

Blues

I got magical powers // defined by skin //
Oh yes I got those magical powers // defined by
skin // It'll make you disappear // this world I'm
living in //

My tongue can dance // dance to a fiddle tune
// Better believe my tongue // can dance to a
fiddle tune // Keep ass-slapping foot-stomping
time // with a shit-faced moon //

To live as they do // an elder to this tribe //
To live as they do // in the end be an elder to
this tribe // Husbandry debts forgiven // my
burial mound left unscribed //

Joke

at the Sandbar near Mandan
the Captains remind the audience

we'll be here all Winter

Travels in North America

To reach the _____, take State Route ____. The best way to view the _____ is from _____. _____ have been restored and are open for public tours.

Course & Distance #04

	Lewis & Clark	Me
Camp Wood	1803.12.12-1804.05.14	2013.07.05
Council Bluff	1804.07.30-08.03	2013.07.07
Floyd's Grave	1804.08.20	2013.07.08
Spirit Mound	1804.08.25	2013.07.09
Fort Mandan	1804.11.03-1805.04.07	2013.07.11
Yellowstone confluence	1805.04.26, 1806	1979.08
Missouri Breaks	1805.05	1986.09
Great Falls	1805.06.16-22	1986.09
Gates of the Mountain	1805.07.19	2010.08.03
Three Forks	1805.07.25-30	1978.06
Bozeman Pass	1806.07.15 (Clark)	1978.06
Pompey's Pillar	1806.07.25	1978.08
Lolo Pass	1805.09.13	2010.08.06
Canoe Camp	1805.09.26-10.07	2010.08.06
Columbia (Snake confluence)	1805.10.16	1986.06
"Ocian in view!" (Astoria)	1805.11.07	1992.06.20
Fort Clatsop	1805.12.07-1806.03.23	2005.09

Sonnet

the leaves of all the trees
                    is now fallen
                    except

                    a tree (an oak

which Stands
                alone
                to make them brave

at Day light it began to *Snow*
& continued all
the fore part of
the Day

                        the leaves of the trees die

& have now fallen
                    the Snow did not lye

Sonnet

wrote untill verry late at night but
little time to devote to my friends

the river is falling fast

        men building perogus,
          makeing ropes, Burning
            coal, Hanging up meat

makeing battle axes for corn

     all the birds
       that we believe visit
          this country have
         now returned

Smoked a pipe with himself and Several old men

but fiew nights pass without a Dance

Lewis & Clark among the Indians

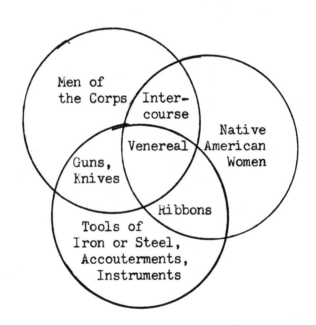

DISPATCH

Thru narrow windows the Captains, who collected Field notes & sketched maps, watched the Party on the parade field.

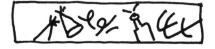

DISPATCH

His exhibited side effects included fever & profuse sweats.

SYPHILIS SPIROCHTE

DISPATCH

Joke

when the Party moves indoors

only the Captains return to the keelboat

with Seaman

Sonnet

Some men went out to hunt & others

      to Dancing

I imploy myself
    making a Small map
    of Connection &c.

I am much engaged
making descriptive
    a List of Rivers
    from Information

I commence a Map
of the Countrey &
its waters &c.

      the ice   began to break
                                    away

Sonnet

I am verry unwelle for want of sleep

>   at Dark
>   as last night
>   the Dance begins

>   they perce
ther flesh w/ arrows above & below
ther elbows
as testimony of ther grief

I came here
naked
& must return home

naked

>   Deturmined to Sleep
>   at last Some

Lewis & Clark among the Indians

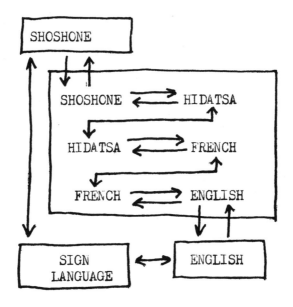

Joke

the Captains have this Interpreter so when the Natives say

"eat shit and die you miserable bastards" they hear

"we beseech you sleep with our Missouri wives"

Notes: *"Winter Fort ..."*

1. Reference is to the Journalist's penis, when noted, "If it still burns when urinated I will see about the slight discharge etc. at the end of winter." Unprotected intercourse was at the time rampant in the Americas.

2. Bunker comrades were routinely treated for venereals, according to the notebook.

Course & Distance #05

Travels in North America

Driving _____ from _____ on Interstate ____, you first pass _____. In spite of its name, _____ is not _____. Turn left on _____ that heads to two monuments erected on a bluff overlooking the _____.

DISPATCH

Snow so insistent the Captains could feel only the closest body.

MERI... IS THAT YOU?

DISPATCH

Eating bear meat caused him to speak of things his Grandfather had said.

> IT WOULD BE TOUGHER IF YOU DIDN'T HAVE ANY...

Course & Distance #06

5 truths about maps:

1. Acceptable maps usually include a key showing the symbols used and their meaning.

2. All maps must show a scale to be of use.

3. Boundaries of many types are shown on maps.

4. Some maps will show distance correctly, others will show angles (hence, course to steer), others will give a better idea as to outlines.

5. Maps need not show that which is visible.

Travels in North America

Today, you can still enjoy _____. After a few miles you'll suddenly find yourself in _____. Archaeologists have done extensive digging a few miles north of _____ in area now administered by _____.

Riff

i.
(fell in w/) 2 brown or yellow
the largest brown (turned on him)

(pursued him) large brown large white
or reather brown (crept on one w/ in 20 step)

ii.
a uniform pale reddish brown
one very nearly white (the Natives

& French call white) the white the deep
& pale red grizzle (forgotten to reload)

iii.
the dark bron grizzle white or frost poil
(300 paces from the river) black w/

white breast uniform bey brown & light
reddish brown (shot) (killed)

Inventory

Essentials for a mountain man, c. 1806

Flintlock rifle, powder horn + lead, Spanish dagger, possible sack w/ extra flints, steel + lead, needle + thread, pipe + tobacco, 8-inch scalping knife, handkerchief + beads, colored glass, brass combs, large Tomahawk aka Missouri war hatchet, fringed buckskin, wolfskin hat + animal-skin poncho, buffalo-robe coat,

Inventory

What I found at a craft fair, Seattle, c. 2008

bent wire silver + copper, bead-strung strings, Far East silk woven, curious spices for steep, buttons, shell + bone, glass + wax, roots, berries, preserves, coastal burls carved or whaled, soaps, stretched + dried sweets, cut bunch grasses, brass fasteners, Navel pins, sea-faring trunk, yellowed almanac, knitted + woolen goods,

Lewis & Clark among the Indians

buffalo buffalo buffalo buffalo
buffalo buffalo buffalo buffalo
buffalo buffalo buffalo buffalo
buffalo buffalo buffalo buffalo
buffalo buffalo buffalo buffalo
buffalo buffalo buffalo buffalo
buffalo buffalo buffalo buffalo
buffalo buffalo buffalo buffalo
buffalo buffalo buffalo buffalo
buffalo buffalo buffalo buffalo
buffalo buffalo buffalo buffalo
buffalo buffalo buffalo buffalo

American

Substitution

for mosquito(es), substitute terrorist(s)

i.
<u>terrorists</u> extremely troublesome insomuch that
without the protection of my <u>terrorist</u> bier I
should have found it impossible to wright a
moment

ii.
the <u>terrorists</u> continue to infest us in Such
manner that we can Scarcely exist; for my own
part I am confined by them ... at least 3/4ths of
my time

iii.
my dog even howls with the torture he
experiences from <u>terrorists</u> ... they are So
numerous that we frequently get <u>terrorists</u> in our
thrats as we breath

iv.
we found the <u>terrorists</u> extremely troublesome
but in this rispect there is but little choice of
camps

v.
<u>terrorists</u> excessively troublesome So much So
that the men complained that they could not
work at their skins ... those <u>terrorists</u> being So
numerous & tormenting as to render it
impossible for a man to continue in the timbered
lands

Travels in North America

Technically, it's not quite true that _____.
The _____ is known principally for its
_____. It's good to spend some time here
because _____ and _____.

Sonnet

Saw great numbers of Gees

Saw flowers in the Prairies

Saw more bald Eagles than usial
    also a Small Hawk

Saw the remains of Indian camps
    after sunset

Saw some fresh Indian tracks
    Some verry large beaver
    taken this morning

Saw a Curlow
            a Gange of brant pass

Saw Several sitting on the bank
    near the waters edge
    in the Prairies, on the young grass

Sonnet

to behold the trees
        Green

    and flowers
spread on the Plains

& Snow an inch deep

to behold
    3 pieces of Scarlet
    one brace in each

to behold
    a Sacrifice
    a curious collection of bushes
    tied up in the shape of a fascene

        to behold
        this offering

Joke

a lawyer, a politician, and the Captains are in a pirogue

the lawyer says so Sieoux me, or is that Seoux me

Lewis & Clark among the Indians

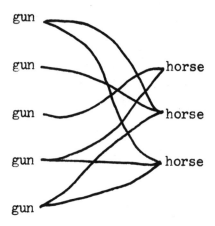

Notes: "*On the Plains ...*"

1. Almost certainly *Bison bison*, aka American buffalo. The Journalist traveled the Yellowstone each March to greet the herd before dispersal to higher grounds.

2. There is no record of surprise in the entry, "A bear crossed the Frontage Road just in front of the Party." Most likely *Ursus americanus*, which is native to North America and at the time of the Journalist's travels had been reclaiming its range, often then subdivisions.

Pacific Coast

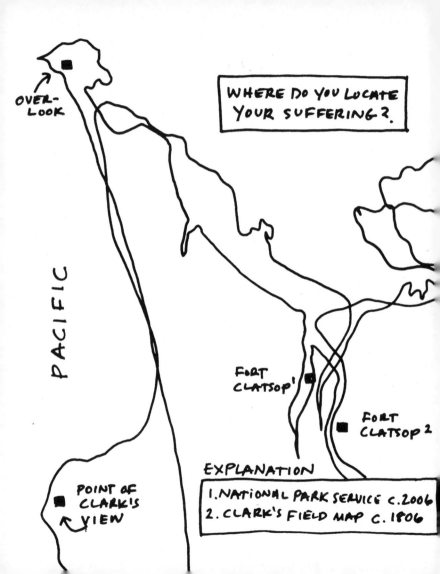

Divine the Source, the tidal wave; Joy roll forth in froth, in song.

Have I sung of the moon, Gregorian tracked, a waning gibbous tonight?

Understand, not only the cause of suffering, but also the means for putting an end to all sufferings.

Pissing beneath a cedar at midnite by the silver of a drunken moon, I hear the Sea roaring its name – foam of white noise heaving heavenward in crescendo of eternity, but enough about the moon.

There is perpetual sadness in the concrete, in a) washed-ashore sterling, b) rusted steel hardware, c) long-rotted docks.

As Theodore Winthrop noted, "Poet comes long after pioneer."

(for this is) time / timing, rhyme / rhyming.

A man is traveling westward desiring to go many thousands of miles ...

History is short, memory shorter.

W A A A A A A A A A K E – up up up up up up up up up (2X).

Camped at Pacific Ocean, 2011.08.16-19.

Course & Distance #07

It's 786.3 miles from Bozeman MT to Orcas Island in the Strait of Juan de Fuca at the north opening of Puget Sound.

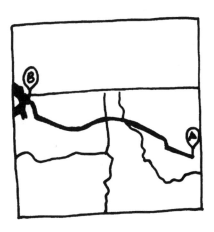

We leave Montana in a snowstorm in March 1984 for the Coast in a 1969 Ford Bronco. We cross four passes: Homestake on the Continental Divide, Lookout on the Montana-Idaho border and Mountain-Pacific time zone, Fourth of July east of Coeur d'Alene, and Snoqualmie Pass through the Cascades coastal range.

Our homestead is a 2nd floor apartment in a complex settled among tall cedars on the north shore of a landmass "shaped like a pair of saddlebags." It's an elevation drop of 4,471 feet to sea level.

Travels in North America

As you continue _____ on Route ____,
look for the turn-off to _____. For a while
_____ was a _____ center, but
there's no trace of it now. Besides the _____,
the principal tourist attraction is _____,
operated by _____.

Blues

I'm gathering up I'm carrying // my burden
another day // Yes I'm gathering him up // said
I carry my burden another day // I keep a tight
hold for those things // trying to float away //

I know about a hard life // though you say I'm
young // You know I know about a hard life //
though you say I'm young // I'll be that lost coda
to your song // I'll be what you leave unsung //

I'm proceeding on // on down thru all this
misery // You see I'm proceeding on // on down
thru all this damn misery // I struggle to
interpret // all these feelings being lonely //

DISPATCH

By the time they reached the Coast their supplies were dwindled til only a few burdens remained.

SACAJAWEA & POMPEY →

DISPATCH

DISPATCH

He takes refuge in the tender subculture of an inexperienced continent.

DISMAL NITCH

Riff

i.
rained all the after rain we are all wet
our Situation is truly disagreeable one

we are all wet as usial distressing to See
our Situation all wet & colde the rain

continues all day all wet rotted nearly
one half of the fiew clothes all wet

& confined to our Shelters we are all wet
our bedding & Stores also wet &c.

ii.
rained all the after rain continues
this morning all wet as usial

great quantities of rain our Situation
all wet & Colde rain continues

all day all wet which has continued
all wet rained all last night

we are all wet proceded on thru
heavy rain gusts of rain Hail & Thunder

iii.
rained all the after slept but
verry little all wet as usial

the great quantities of rain small stones
fall down upon us to see our Situation

distroyed the robes & rotted
all wet continued w/out longer

intermition all wet our bedding & Stores
whorl winds worst day that ever was

Travels in North America

The road along the north side of the river goes
through _____, where _____. It's
good to _____ while you're here.
Historians disagree: _____, _____.

Joke

at the Wine tasting one Captain says
it reminds me of a Drouillard

the other Captain replies that's funny
I thought it was a Charbonneau

Course & Distance #08

8 Ways of Looking at a Dam

i. I remember a garden of stone petroglyphs, rescued before the reservoir filled behind the dam, piled outside the Visitor Center.

ii. The tour boat takes off from the dam and chugs upriver into the Wilderness Area, where over a static-equipped loudspeaker the guide announces this looks pretty much like it did when Lewis & Clark come through here over 200 years ago.

iii. Was Woody Guthrie being ironic when he wrote "Roll On Columbia"?

iv. Of the rivers traveled by the Corps of Discovery only the Yellowstone today remains undammed.

v. Inside the Power House the turbines make a low hum, a vibration felt deep in our guts.

vi. "Our current level of technological development could not have been achieved without the construction of dams."

vii. At night in the summers we are told the concave face of the dam dances with lasers.

viii. How to imagine a cascade or a series of Great Falls beneath the placid surface of the reservoir? How to imagine there is still, deep down there, rushing and foaming and roaring?

Notes: "At the Coast ..."

1. Compare the sentiment "I take the same path every day to always-familiar work" to "the same moon lights everyone's path at night" which the Journalist had translated from the Japanese (*gekko terashi / yube no michi / hitobito iku*) in the margins.

2. "I hear sounds outside my Gate tonite" is most nearly a reference to an obscure passage in <u>The Blue Cliff Record</u>. Historians say a late imprint of this text accompanied the Journalist to the Coast. Note the 46th Case: *Ching Ch'ing asked a monk, "What is the sound outside the Gate?" the monk said, "The sound of raindrops."*

Joke

the Captains walked into this Sports bar
North Dakota Sunday afternoon

they see Buffalo playing

Inventory

Game killed by the expedition as compiled by Raymond Darwin Burroughs, c. 1961

1,001 deer, 357 elk, 227 bison, 62 antelope, 35 bighorned sheep, 43 grizzly bear, 23 black bear, 113 beaver, 16 otter, 104 geese + brant, 45 ducks + coots, 46 grouse, 9 turkeys, 48 plovers, 18 wolves, 12 horses, 190 dogs

Inventory

Uses made of buffalo, Akta Lakota Museum poster, c. 2013

for totem, for clan, for meat (every part), horn for cups + spoons, hair + beard for ornamentation, hide for buckskin + rawhide, for moccasins + robe, muscle for sinew, skull for ceremony, bones for tools, hoof + feet for rattles, scrotum for rattle, bladder for medicine bag, stomach for vessel, tail for a medicine switch,

Joke

the Captains pull a prairie dog and four magpies
out of their trunk

for their second act they pull Cruzette out of
their ass

Lewis & Clark among the Indians

                    Ordway

         Drouillard
              Lewis

                                    Field
                                    Field

     Blackfeet   Blackfeet
                      Blackfeet

        Bla☒feet
                         Blackfeet

     Blackfeet
        Blackfeet
                              Bla☒feet

Riff

i.
how great the destruction
we have seen floating 8 Buffaloes

their bodies have been known to pass
swollen & putrid, the city of St. Louis

only a few pieces from the young bull
& its tongue, were brought on board

men being too lazy, or too far off
to cut out even the tongues of others

ii.
enormous carcasses are suffered to be
prey of the Wolf, the Raven, the Buzzard

as the tongues only were brought in
only its tongue, brought on board

only a few pieces from the young bull
prairies literally covered with their skulls

as if it were for nothing, or next to it
to rot in the spots where they fell

iii.
their bodies known to pass St. Louis
even now a perceptible difference

its tongue, as the tongues only were taken
were for nothing, swollen & putrid

only a few pieces from a young bull
thousands murdered in senseless play

even now the size of the herd
& the flesh of the animals was left

Lewis & Clark among the Indians

of what the old
man said
No journalist recorded
The concern

Course & Distance #09

There are three landscapes that have left me with a feeling of aloneness, reminded me of my insignificance and /or asserted the certainty of death:
      1. The Valley of the Three Forks
      2. The Pacific Ocean
      3. The Great Plains of the Dakotas

Sonnet

I crossed
I assended
I viewed
I held
I have always held
    for the first time
    with Certainty

I could only
I found
I will allow I felt
    a secret pleasure
    so near the head
    of the heretofore
    conceived boundless

Sonnet

I counter ballanced the joy
in the first moments
to anticipate
a fiew of the most elivated
          points
        above

I reflect on the difficulties
and the Sufferings
and hardships

    in the first
    moments

    I will allow
    it to be
    otherwise—

Substitution

for buffalo(s), substitute hippie(s)

i.
the open bottoms border on the hills, and are
covered in many parts by the wild hyssop which
rises to the hight of two feet. I observe the
<u>hippies</u> feed on this herb;

ii.
2 <u>hippies</u> were near the water at the time of
dineing ... I also saw several parsels of <u>hippies'</u>
hair hanging on the rose bushes, which had been
bleached by exposure to the weather and became
perfectly white.

iii.
walking on shore this evening I met with a <u>hippie</u>
which attached itself to me and continued to

follow close at my heels until I embarked and left it. the <u>hippie</u> appeared alarmed at my dog

iv.
the <u>hippies</u> are so gentle that we pass near them while feeding, without appearing to excite any alarm among them, and when we attract their attention, <u>hippies</u> frequently approach us more nearly to discover what we are, and in some instances pursue us a considerable distance

v.
I Saw immence quantities of <u>hippies</u> in every direction; they are extremely gentle. the bull <u>hippie</u> particularly will scarcely give way to you. I passed several in the open plains within fifty paces, they viewed me for a moment as something novel and then very unconcernedly continued

Travels in North America

The more interesting things to see and do in
_____ are near _____. The
_____, a kind of _____, is being
refurbished along the lines of _____.
The drive north through the _____ is
through pleasant, undulating hills.

DISPATCH

His dreams were filled with interconnected rooms that vaguely felt like home.

Travels in North America

You can see some nice _____ by turning _____ on State Highway _____ and driving to _____. _____ now has two shopping centers, one north and one south of town. As you drive west from _____, Main Street soon joins _____, which then becomes State Highway _____.

Blues

Tonite's my journal's finished // my ink just about gone // Tonite don't say my journal's finished // my ink just about gone // Pierced and bleeding I wait // I wait for this slow dawn //

My head is rushing // roaring like some great falls // Can't you hear my head it's rushing // roaring like some great falls // There are no laws // nothing Philosophical left at all //

I'm done with this sublunary world // done with all its sin // Believe me I'm done with this sublunary world // I'm done with all its sin // Oh I'm lying down a last time // on these robes of buffalo skin //

Notes: *"Returning ..."*

1. Most likely the Blackfeet Reservation on the edge of the present-day Wilderness Area. The Journalist was known to take long weekends in search of solitude & visions, and would often learn the kitchen was closed.

2. "Hawks circle my camp" is the most politically charged entry from the Journalist at the time of his writing. For the most part, this comment appears to be an exception to the notebook, which seldom records sentiment from his punk days.

St. Louis

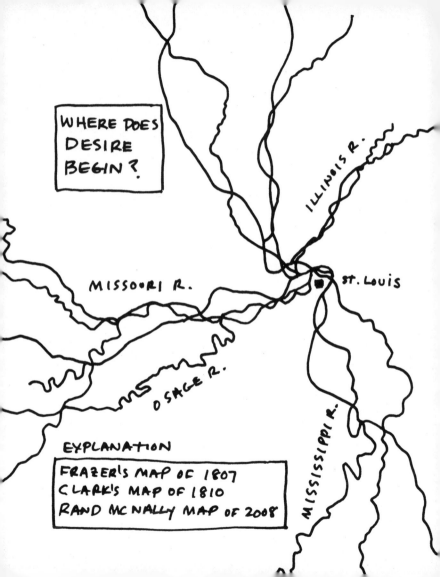

When I stand where everything begins, where rivers meet, what do I record?

If fortification is added, does a camp or village become a fort, and what are the anthropological presumptions informing that designation?

In what ways are the boarded-up houses and vacant lots of North St. Louis like the abandoned Mandan village at Double Ditch?

Where we walk, what are walking over?

How does your perspective change by climbing even the slightest mound while on the Great Plains?

How many quarters does it take to win the Golden Buffalo?

How does the word "encounter" take on contextual significance when asking a Sioux street artist about the meaning symbolized in his paintings and wondering how long tattoos have marked members of the tribe?

What are the characteristics of a) prairie grass that make it a good place for taking a piss; b) sandbars that they remain useful, while not permanent, to citizens of the river?

Does size matter when evaluating the effectiveness of river transportation and functionality as in canoe, pirogue, keelboat and riverboat?

True or False: Desire's only concern is what was or what might be?

Camped along L&C trail, St. Louis to Bismarck, 2013.07.04-12.

Inventory

from Charter of the Philosophical
Society, Philadelphia, c. 1769

Newly discovered plants, herbs, trees,
roots, their virtues, uses &c.
improvements of vegetable juices,
such as ciders, wines &c.
improvements in any branch of
Mathematics, new arts, trades
& Manufacturers &c. surveys,
maps & charts, all philosophical experiments that let light
into the Nature of things,

Inventory

Dams currently along the water course of the Lewis & Clark expedition, compiled c. 2013

Gavins Point, Fort Randall, Big Bend, Oahe, Garrison, Fort Peck, Morony, Ryan, Cochrane, Rainbow, Black Eagle, Holter, Hauser, Canyon Ferry, Toston, Little Goose, Lower Monumental, Ice Harbor, McNary, John Day, The Dalles, Bonneville,

Joke

So the Sergeant's account is published first

at the book signing the Captains keep passing
Gass

Lewis & Clark among the Indians

1. skillfully   a. grasped

2. eagerly   b. thwarted

3. quickly   c. abandoned

4. closely   d. discovered

5. faithfully   e. colored

6. failed   f. and shot

DISPATCH

Submerged in riverfront applause the Captains waved their hats in return.

DISPATCH

> He kept a flintlock long rifle, split thru the stock, rested beneath his wedded bed of pelts, skins & robes.

DISPATCH

A fine morning we commenced wrighting &c.

MMM... I WONDER WHAT TO TELL YOU.

Course & Distance #10

Did you expect a narrative? Events aren't always remembered chronologically. Stories are often just leftover feelings, fragments, giving you a sense or an intuition with no linear logic. Incidents are recalled very differently by witnesses and later put back together in many different orders by reconstructionists, interpreters and journalists. Let's start all over again ...

Did you expect a narrative?

1. My dad died when I was 10 from a coronary late one Sunday evening in June 1968 in upstate NY.

2. I carry with me things that belonged to him as deer hunter, outdoorsman, surveyor and draftsman.

3. As a teenager I took solace in the woods, walking alone, sitting beneath the deciduous, later learning the stars and constellations, the name of plants and trees, camping and hiking, reading Thoreau and Emerson.

4. I learned to keep my feelings to myself.

5. Ever since I was 17, I have written in a notebook, which later became wrapped in Rising Sun leather that still covers it today.

6. When I arrived in Montana in 1978 to work on a crew of land surveyors my aunt was dying of cancer.

7. The Journals of Lewis & Clark accompanied me as eager journalist and new pioneer enamored with surveyors, maps, the mythic West and what had been lost and later a homesteader proceeding on to the Coast.

8. We buried my aunt at Mt. View in March of 1980 when there was still a blanket of snow covering the Gallatin Valley. Her plot located in the NE quadrant of the cemetery facing the Bridgers remains mostly unattended.

9. Sometimes all I am left with for certainty is what I feel to be true or true enough, or what I desire to be true – trusting in the physicality of the artifacts I carry with me, rereading journals, visiting historical sites and markers, relocating what's lost to time and neglect.

10. You're standing where the dam broke.

Sources

For this is the era of the description of the All
—*Ed Sanders*

THE JOURNALS

The Journals of Lewis and Clark, John Bakeless, editor (Mentor, 1964).

The Lewis and Clark Journals: An American Epic of Discovery, Gary E. Moulton, editor (University of Nebraska Press, 2003).

The Definitive Journals of Lewis & Clark, Volumes 1-13, Gary E. Moulton, editor (University of Nebraska Press, 2003).

Original Journals of the Lewis & Clark Expedition, Volume 8, Reuben Gold Thwaites, editor (Arno Press, 1969).

The Journals of the Expedition under the command of Capts. Lewis and Clark, Volumes 1 and 2, Nicholas Biddle, editor (The Heritage Press, 1962).

HISTORY BOOKS

A History of the Lewis and Clark Journals, Paul Russell Cutright (University of Oklahoma Press, 1976).

Lewis & Clark among the Indians, James P. Ronda (University of Nebraska Press, 1984).

Lewis and Clark in the Three Rivers Valley, Donald F. Nell and John E. Taylor (Headwaters Chapter Lewis & Clark Trail Heritage Foundations and The Patrice Press, Tucson, Arizona, 1996).

Lewis and Clark in North Dakota, Russell Reid (State Historical Society of North Dakota, Bismarck, ND, 1948 and 1988).

Lewis & Clark: Pioneering Naturalists, Paul Russell Cutright (University of Nebraska Press, 1969).

Lewis & Clark: The Journey of the Corps of Discovery, Dayton Duncan and Ken Burns (A Borzoi Book, Alfred A. Knopf, 1997).

Ocian in view! O! the Joy: Lewis & Clark in Washington State, Robert C. Carriker (Washington State Historical Society, 2005).

Only One Man Died: The Medical Aspects of the Lewis and Clark Expedition, E.G. Chuinard, M.D. (Ye Galleon Press, Fairfield, Washington, 1979).

The Adventures of Lewis and Clark, Ormonde de Kay, Jr. (Step Up Books, Random House, 1968).

The Fate of the Corps, Larry E. Morris (Yale University Press, 2004).

The Lolo Trail, Ralph S. Space (Historic Montana Publishing, Missoula, Montana, 2001).

The Men of the Lewis & Clark Expedition, Charles G. Clarke (University of Nebraska Press, 1970).

The Natural History of the Lewis and Clark Expedition, Raymond Darwin Burroughs (Michigan State University Press, 1995).

To the Pacific with Lewis and Clark, Ralph K. Andrist (Harper & Row, 1967).

Undaunted Courage, Stephen E. Ambrose (Touchstone, 1996) and audio version (Audioworks).

We Proceeded On, November 2001 (The Lewis and Clark Trail Heritage Foundation).

TRAVEL GUIDES

Fielding's Lewis & Clark Trail, Gerald Olmsted (Fielding Travel Books, 1986).

Going Along with Lewis & Clark, Barbara Fifer (Montana Magazine, 2000).

Lewis & Clark: Historic Places Associated with Their Transcontinental Exploration (1804-06), Roy E. Appleman (United States Department of the Interior National Park Service, Washington, D.C.,1975).

Passage of Discovery: The American Rivers Guide to the Missouri River of Lewis and Clark, Daniel B. Botkin (Penguin Putnam, 1999).

The Lewis & Clark Trail, Thomas Schmidt (National Geographic Society, 1998).

The Traveler's Guide to the Lewis & Clark Trail, Julie Fanselow (Falcon Press Publishing, Helena, Montana, 1994).

MISCELLANY

Benjamin Franklin: An American Life, Walter Isaacson (Simon & Schuster, 1996).

Indian Rock Art of the Columbia Plateau, James D. Keyser (University of Washington Press, 1992).

On Sacred Ground: The Spirit of Place in Pacific Northwest Literature, Nicholas O'Connell (University of Washington Press, 2003).

Oregon Geographic Names, Lewis A. McArthur (Binfords & Mort, 1928 and 1965).

River of the West: A Chronicle of the Columbia, Robert Clark (Picador, 1995).

The Crow and the Eagle: A Tribal History from Lewis & Clark to Custer, Keith Algier (The Caxton Printers, Caldwell, Idaho, 1993).

The Dam Book, George Sainsbuy and Nanci Hertzog (Klatawa Enterprises, 1970).

The Journey of York, Frank X. Walker (The University Press of Kentucky, 2004).

The Last Best Place: A Montana Anthology, William Kittredge and Annick Smith, editors (Falcon Press, 1988)